Live the
Little Way

*A Practical Guide to Living
the Little Way of Spiritual Childhood*

by

Susan Brinkmann, OCDS

CATHOLIC LIFE INSTITUTE

P R E S S

P.O. Box 1173
Pottstown, PA 19464

NIHIL OBSTAT:
Robert A. Pesarchick, STD, STL, MA, M.Div

IMPRIMATUR:
Archbishop Charles J. Chaput, OFM Cap.
No. 00012, April 12, 2019

Catholic Life Institute Press

PO Box 1173 Pottstown, PA 19464

Cover Design by IGD Graphic Design, www.image-gd.com
Interior Layout by Elizabeth Racine, www.ElizabethRacine.com

Live the Little Way/ Susan Brinkmann. -- 1st ed.
ISBN-13: 978-1-7336724-2-9

*"No, I don't believe I'm a great saint;
I believe I'm a very little saint;
but I think God has been pleased to
place things in me which will do good
to me and to others."*

-St. Thérèse of Lisieux

Live the Little Way!
Sue Brinkman

Born 1·2·1873
Entered Carmel 9·8·1890
BVM Birthday
Died 9·30·1897
Age 24

Prayer to St. Thérèse
as
Queen of the Very Little Ones
(*Reine des Tout-Petits*)

St. Thérèse, Queen of the Very Little Ones, thank you for bringing me to this moment in my life. I am a very little one who never thought I had a chance at sainthood until you showed me your Little Way.

Please be with me in a special way as I ponder your wisdom. Intercede for me before God that He might remove all that prevents me from fully embracing your Way of humility, trust, and abandonment.

Help me to be open to your teachings like never before so that I might learn to love my littleness, to become full of confidence in the mercy of God, and to abandon my life to Him as you did when you lived upon the earth.

Embrace me as one of your very little ones, form me in the Little Way of Spiritual Childhood, and enable me to share in your mission to make God loved in this world.

I ask all this in the most Holy Name of Jesus, through the intercession of Our Lady of Mount Carmel.

Amen.

CONTENTS

A Short Biography of
St. Thérèse of Lisieux

Marie-Francois Thérèse Martin was born on January 2, 1873, in Alencon, France. The youngest of five girls born to the Martins, she was blonde, blue-eyed, precocious, lively, very touchy, capable of violent outbursts of temper, and stubborn.

And because she was the favorite of her father, who referred to her as his "little queen," she was also quite spoiled.

The death of her mother from breast cancer when she was just 4 years old began a dark period in her life

In her diary, *Story of a Soul*, she says she didn't cry much on the day her mother died, but she would do little else for the next 10 years of her life - from the age of four until she was 14 - which she referred to in her diary as "the most painful" of her years on earth.

As she would write about herself: " . . . (M)y happy disposition completely changed after Mamma's death. I, once so full of life, became timid and retiring, sensitive to an excessive degree. One look was enough to reduce me to tears, and the only way I was content was to be left alone completely. I could not bear the company of strangers and found my joy only within the intimacy of the family."[1]

During this time, her father moved the family from Alencon to Les Buissonnets, a home she greatly loved.

Even from a young age, she was always awed and amazed with God. A natural contemplative, as most children are, she would often sit in the fields and think of heaven.

---

1 St. Thérèse of Lisieux, *Story of a Soul*, translated by John Clarke, OCD (Washington DC: ICS Publications, 1972) pg. 34

During visits to the Blessed Sacrament, she loved to sit in the "deep dark quiet" of the Church and ponder that "Divine Prisoner of Love" who confined Himself to a little metal box just so He could be available when someone might need Him.

Later, when she went to school, she had a difficult time making friends and would often sit in the chapel beside the tabernacle, wherein lived "Her only friend."

It's no wonder that on her first Communion Day, she wept with joy after making her first physical contact with "her only friend" - people thought she was crying for her mother - but these were tears of joy.

"How sweet was that first kiss of Jesus . . ." she wrote. "Thérèse had vanished as a drop of water is lost in the immensity of the ocean. Jesus alone remained."[2]

Physically, Thérèse was never well. She complained throughout those ten years of stomach pains and headaches. Being so sensitive, she was also left distraught at this time over the vocations of her older sisters Marie and Pauline who became Carmelite nuns. In her childlike eyes, they were leaving her just like her mother had left and this was all too much for her.

This all came to a head in 1883 when, while she was staying with her cousins, she began to suffer a constant headache that gradually became worse until she was suffering from hallucinations, fits of fever, trembling, and delirium. Experts have diagnosed her sickness as everything from a nervous breakdown to a kidney infection.

Thérèse blamed it on the devil. Whatever it was, doctors of her time were unable to either diagnose or treat it.

"I was absolutely terrified by everything: my bed seemed to be surrounded by frightful precipices; some nails in the wall of the room took on the appearance of big black charred fingers, making me cry out in fear. One day, while Papa was looking at me and smiling, the hat in his hand was suddenly transformed into some indescribable dreadful shape and I showed such great fear that poor Papa left the room sobbing."[3]

---

2 *Story of a Soul*, pg. 77
3 *Story of a Soul*, footnote No. 56, pg. 63

Nothing the doctors did helped. Finally, on May 13, 1883, out of sheer desperation, her sisters knelt in front of a statue of Our Lady - now famously known as "Our Lady of the Smile" - and begged for their little sister's life. As they prayed, Thérèse turned toward the statue and prayed for a cure.

Suddenly, the statue became ravishingly beautiful. "I had never seen anything so beautiful. Her face exuded an inexpressible kindness and tenderness, but what pierced me to the depths of my soul was the Virgin's ravishing smile. Then, all my pain vanished, and two great tears fell from my eyes, and flowed silently over my cheeks, but they were tears of unalloyed joy ... Ah, I said to myself, the Blessed Virgin has smiled at me. How happy I am! ... But I won't tell anyone, because then my happiness would disappear."[4]

Thérèse was cured.

But all was not well for long. Shortly after her confirmation, she entered a period of 17 months during which time she suffered a particularly cruel attack of scruples. She lived in constant fear of sinning; the most abhorrent and absurd thoughts disturbed her peace. She wept often.

"I was really unbearable because of my extreme touchiness," she was to write later. "If I happened to cause anyone I loved some little trouble, even unwittingly, instead of forgetting about it and not crying, which made matters worse, I cried like a Magdalene and then when I began to cheer up, I'd begin to cry again for having cried."[5]

Then came the infamous Christmas grace of 1886 which she experienced after Midnight Mass on Christmas. The Lord stripped away all of her scruples and over-sensitivity, the self-doubt, the depression, the uncertainty, and replaced it with a new calm and inner conviction.

She would use this grace as the fuel to get her through the next big battle of her life, which was to gain entrance to Carmel at the tender age of 15.

---

4 Ibid, pg. 66
5 Ibid, pg. 97

With her typical stubbornness, she pursued this dream all the way to Rome where she knelt at the feet of Pope Leo XIII and, disobeying orders that visitors were not to speak during the audience, she blurted out her desires to enter Carmel at 16. He told her to obey her Superiors – who were already considering the idea but had not yet come to a decision.

Her impertinence paid off. Sr. Thérèse of the Holy Child Jesus and the Holy Face made her solemn profession at the Lisieux Carmel on the feast of Our Lady's birthday, September 8, 1890.

During her time in Carmel, where she was joined by three of her sisters, she experienced a loss of all consolation in prayer and spent those years in the aridity of the desert in a spiritual sense.

Life in the Carmel had its share of problems such as the cold, the new diet and the difficulties of prayer which demanded up to six hours a day.

But it was community life where Thérèse developed her Little Way. Because she did not have the physical or emotional countenance to withstand great fasts and hair shirts, she had to make do with what she could do.

For example, she made a penance out of ignoring a nun who continually splashed water in her face during communal laundering.

Another nun would click her ill-fitting dentures during prayer which so distracted her the only way she could keep her mind was to secretly make a concert out of the noise and offer it to Jesus.

Then there was the crotchety old nun who did nothing but complain no matter what Thérèse did to help her.

Her personal weaknesses were also a plague. For example, she often fell asleep in prayer, which really embarrassed her. However, in what is one of her most charming expressions of the Little Way, she realized one day that parents love their children just as much while asleep as awake, so God loved her even though she often slept during the time for prayers.

Before her death on September 30, 1897, she would sum up her Little Way of Spiritual Childhood in this famous paragraph:

"Spiritual childhood is the way of confidence and abandonment . . . It means that we acknowledge our nothingness; that we expect everything from the good Lord, as a child expects everything from its father; it means to worry about nothing, not to build upon fortune; it means to remain little, seeking only to gather flowers, the flowers of sacrifice, and to offer them to the good Lord for His pleasure. It also means not to attribute to ourselves the virtues we practice, not to believe we are capable of anything, but to acknowledge that it is the good Lord who has placed that treasure in the hand of His little child that He may use it when He needs it, but it remains always God's own treasure. Finally, it means that we must not be discouraged by our faults, for children fall frequently."[6]

During the course of this study, we will unpack three of the most essential points in this paragraph which are considered to be the core elements of Spiritual Childhood – humility, confidence, and abandonment.

---

6 Clarke, John OCD, *St. Thérèse of Lisieux: Her Last Conversations* (Washington, DC: *ICS Publications*) 1972, pg. 138

An Overview

It has been more than 100 years since the death of St. Thérèse of the Child Jesus and the Holy Face, more affectionately known as the Little Flower of Lisieux, but her legacy is stronger than ever. In addition to her heralded "shower of roses" that have strewn countless miracles throughout the world since her death in 1897, her spiritual doctrine, known as the Little Way of Spiritual Childhood, has inspired some of the greatest saints of modern times – such as St. Pio of Pietrelcina, St. John Paul II, and St. Teresa of Calcutta. But the true wonder of the Little Way is how it has endeared itself to the common folk, giving them a simple road map to follow that will bring them to the same heights of holiness as a St. Francis of Assisi or a St. Catherine of Siena.

However, it's important to understand from the very start that just because her spiritual doctrine is called the Little Way of Spiritual Childhood doesn't mean it's inferior to the teachings of the great mystical giants of our Church. Indeed, she was a student of St. John of the Cross, a Carmelite and Doctor of the Church who lived in Spain during the 16th Century and left us some of the most profound teachings on Catholic mysticism ever recorded.

Like Thérèse, St. John also taught about the primacy of love in one's relationship with God, about the need to strip oneself of everything that is not of God, and the necessity to acquire the kind of confidence founded upon the virtue of hope that makes blind faith possible. But St. John's theology is very deep, his language austere. Thérèse approaches the same subjects from a completely different vantage point – that of the "little ones."

"She is a young teacher who sits down near us to tell us her experiences. She is only a little doctor with notions so simple they seem poor," writes P. Marie-Eugene, OCD.[7]

Her notions are anything but poor!

Nor are they childish, which too many mistakenly believe. Rather, the Little Way of Spiritual Childhood is an attitude of mind and heart.

When asked to explain what she meant by the words "to remain as a little child before God," she said:

"'It is to recognize our nothingness, to look for everything from God as a little child looks for everything from his father; it is to be disquieted about nothing, and not to be set on gaining our fortune . . . To be little, moreover, is not to attribute to ourselves the virtues we practice, nor to believe ourselves capable of practicing virtue at all. It is, rather, to recognize the fact that God puts treasures of virtue into the hands of His little children to make use of them in time of need, but they remain always treasures of the good God'."[8]

These seemingly simple words contain all of the most profound truths of the spiritual life – the need to be humble before God, to be utterly poor in spirit and to rely upon Him for everything with the kind of confidence that can only be found in a faith firmly grounded in hope.

Jesus Himself enunciated these truths and indicated the need for a spiritual childhood when He told Nicodemus that he must be reborn in the Spirit.

"Amen, amen I say to you, no one can enter the Kingdom of God without being born of water and the Spirit."[9]

---

7 P. Marie-Eugene, OCD, *I Am a Daughter of the Church: A Practical Synthesis of Carmelite Spirituality*, Vol. II, Translated by Sister M. Verda Clare, CSC (Allen, TX: *Christian Classics*, 1997) pg. 389.
8 *St. Thérèse of Lisieux: Her Last Conversations*, translated by John Clarke, OCD (Washington, DC: *ICS Publications*, 1977, pg. 138
9 John 3:5

A man cannot be reborn of the Spirit unless he is poor, trusting, and dependent in all things on God.

As the spiritual masters teach us, " . . . [T]o be reborn is nothing else than progressively to become a child. While in the material order generation, realized in the womb of the mother, comes to its perfection in a progressive separation of the child until it can live its perfect and independent life, a spiritual generation comes about inversely by a progressive absorption into unity."[10]
In other words, in the physical life a man grows larger and stronger and more self-reliant as he matures. In the spiritual life, maturation occurs by growing smaller, weaker, and more reliant on God.

This process begins when the sinner is enlightened by God and repents of his sinful and egotistical ways, shuns his inordinate attachment to the material world, and draws closer and closer to the Truth until he loses himself in the God who created him.

"Such is the meaning and the value of spiritual childhood."[11]

But Thérèse was not familiar with teachings as sublime as these when the Little Way first began to take shape in her heart. Instead, this process was born out of her own personal experience with God and how she and her family lived out their faith in everyday life.

Raised in a devout Catholic family, she developed a desire to be a saint at an early age. As she grew, so did this desire; but at the same time, this somewhat spoiled and very pampered little girl realized just how incapable she was of achieving such a lofty goal on her own. In her mind, the kind of sanctity achieved by the saints of old seemed like an impossibly high goal for ordinary people like herself.

But at the same time, she simply could not believe that God would put such a desire into her heart if it was impossible to attain. This simply wasn't the loving Father-God she had come to know. And because she knew that it was impossible to add anything to one's stature, this meant she'd have to accept herself along with

---

10 *I Am a Daughter of the Church*, pg. 399-400
11 *I Am a Daughter of the Church*, pg. 400

her many imperfections. How, then, might she achieve the goal that the good Lord had placed upon her heart?

While pondering this mystery one day, she suddenly recalled how some houses were being outfitted with a new device known as an elevator which allowed the occupants an easy way to reach the upper stories of the house without having to climb stairs. Perhaps there was some sort of "elevator" that she could use that would lift her to the heights of sainthood.

As was her habit, she turned to Holy Scripture and opened to a passage from Proverbs which reads: "Whoever is a little one let him come to me."[12]

From this passage she surmised that in order to attain holiness, one must become little. Further thought revealed that it was necessary to grow in littleness but, because this very littleness makes us incapable of attaining holiness by our own power, we must have recourse to God.

Very well, but what would God do for these little ones who came to Him for help?

It was then that she opened to another verse in Scripture where the Lord answered this question through the mouth of the prophet Isaiah. "You shall be carried at the breasts, and upon the knees they shall caress you."[13]

She suddenly realized what God was trying to teach her – that it would be God Himself who served as the "elevator" for little souls such as herself. If they would only agree to become little – that is, to grow in humility and spiritual poverty by accepting their weaknesses and learning to turn to Him with confidence, He would raise these little ones to the heights of holiness with His own arms.

"Holiness does not consist in this or that practice; it consists in a disposition of the heart, which makes us always humble and little in the arms of God, well aware of our feebleness, but boldly confident in the Father's goodness," she writes. [14]

---

12 Proverbs 9:4

13 Isaiah 66:12

14 *Collected Poems of St. Thérèse of Lisieux,* Translated by Alan Bancroft, (Heredforshire, UK: *Gracewing Publishing* 2001) pg 215

In other words, we must go to God by way of humility, confidence, and abandonment – which is the way of spiritual childhood.

However, this doesn't mean that we do nothing and presume upon God to do it all for us. As Thérèse once taught a novice, we must always do as much as we can on our own.

"You make me think of a little child that is learning to stand but does not yet know how to walk. In his desire to reach the top of the stairs to find his mother, he lifts his little foot to climb the first step. It is all in vain, and at each renewed effort he falls. Well, be like that little child. Always keep lifting your foot to climb the ladder of holiness, and do not imagine that you can mount even the first step. All God asks of you is good will. From the top of the ladder He looks lovingly upon you, and soon, touched by your fruitless efforts, He will Himself come down, and, taking you in His arms, will carry you to His Kingdom never again to leave Him."[15]

We must always do our part but not without accepting the fact that the ascent to holiness is a work only God can do. Our job is to work with Him, to be open to Him, and to always remain confident in His help. Never should we be ashamed of our littleness, of having to depend upon Him; rather we must know that it is this very littleness that attracts God to us.

Being so little can indeed be humiliating. Thérèse had personal experience with this. Even though she was awed by the heroic virtue of the great martyrs of the Church, the little saint of Lisieux once fell sick just from wearing a small iron cross that was studded with sharp points. She believed God allowed this to happen to teach her that the austerities of the Saints were not meant for her – or for the little souls who would one day walk in the path of Spiritual Childhood.

Thus, she learned first-hand that even the highest inspirations don't make one capable of achieving sanctity. No, this is accomplished only through genuine love and the good works that love inspired – whatever good works we are capable of – and a constant dependence on God. Simply desiring the holiness of the saints is not enough. Just like she learned when wearing the iron cross, we must do our

---

15 Quoted in *I Am a Daughter of the Church*, pg. 406

part even if that means coming face-to-face with our own ineptness.

"How many souls plead: 'I have not enough fortitude to accomplish such an act? But let them put forth some effort! The good God never refused the first grace which imparts courage to act. After that, the heart is strengthened, and the soul goes on from victory to victory."[16]

For Thérèse, victory came in the way of little things, sitting up straight in her chair when she felt like slouching; smiling even though she was sad inside; biting back a sour look when annoyed. These little things she could do – with great love. Thus she learned to be content with – and even to love – her littleness.

As the years progressed and Thérèse began to practice the Little Way more and more, she began to realize that this way of spiritual childhood was a "little way – very straight, very short – entirely new."[17]

The way is straight because "it has removed spiritual complexities which were like so many detours in our march toward God."[18]

The way is short "for being straight it simplifies the spiritual life, reducing it especially to humility and confident love."[18]

The way is new "in comparison with the systems which were then in vogue . . ." [20]

New indeed! The prevailing mode of Catholicism that was being practiced in nineteenth-century France at the time of her childhood was known as Jansenism.

As John F. Russell, O.Carm, STD, explains, "Consequently, God appeared more as a just Judge who was punishing France for its

---

16 *I Am a Daughter of the Church*, page 409
17 Quoted by Francois Jamart, OCD, *Complete Spiritual Doctrine of St. Thérèse of Lisieux* (Staten Island, New York: *Alba House*, 1961) pg. 33 [18] Ibid
18 *Complete Spiritual Doctrine of St. Thérèse of Lisieux*, pg. 33 [20] Ibid

sins. The spiritual climate called for reparation, mortifications, prayers offered in atonement."[19]

Thérèse was influenced by this climate, but her own experience with God taught her just the opposite, that God was primarily Love and that all of His other attributes – particularly that of Justice – was mitigated by His mercy.

"'How good is the Lord and His mercy endures forever!' (Ps. 117:1). It seems to me that if all creatures had received the same graces I received, God would be feared by none but would be loved to the point of folly; and through *love*, not through fear, no one would ever consent to cause Him any pain," she writes in the *Story of a Soul*.[20]

"What a sweet joy it is to think that God is *Just*, i.e., that He takes into account our weakness, that He is perfectly aware of our fragile nature. What should I fear then? Ah! Must not the infinitely just God, who deigns to pardon the faults of the prodigal son with so much kindness, be just also toward me who 'am with Him always'?"[21] [*emphasis in original*]

Thus, the Little Way, which she developed over her 24 short years of life, had a very specific intent:

"To reveal God as Love to souls is the central and essential point of the mission of Saint Thérèse of the Child Jesus."[22]

It's interesting to note that Thérèse never intended to write a book about a new spiritual doctrine.

In 1895, about two years before her death, her older sister, Marie, asked the Prioress of the Carmel of Lisieux to allow her little sister to write memoirs of their childhood and youth. Thérèse obeyed and wrote the first eight chapters of what would become The *Story of a Soul* in a notebook. This project was completed in 1896.

---

19 Russell, John T. "Concept of Spiritual Childhood," accessed at http://www.littleflower.org/Thérèse/reflections/st-Thérèse-and-spir-itual-childhood/
20 Story of a Soul, pg. 180
21 Ibid
22 *I am a Daughter of the Church*, pg. 389

Later, Marie asked Thérèse to write down what the young nun, now terminally ill with tuberculosis, referred to her as her "little doctrine." The result became Chapter XI of the same story.

In June of 1897, just a few months before her death, Thérèse was asked to add a description of her religious life, which became Chapters IX and X of *The Story of a Soul*. These last two chapters were written in pencil because Thérèse was too weak to hold a pen.

None of the three manuscripts were ever intended for the public. The first was only for her family, the second was exclusively for Marie, and the third was intended for use by the Convent in writing Thérèse's obituary. This last part was the only one that would be publicly known, and even this would be in a limited manner.

However, it quickly became apparent that many souls would draw profit from the book and Marie did ask her little sister for permission to publish it. Thérèse had no objection and the two revised the final copy.

That her ideas would generate suspicion among her contemporaries, many of whom were still steeped in the strictness of Jansenism, was not lost on Thérèse. In fact, she once told her novices: "If I lead you into error with my Little Way of Love, be not afraid that I shall permit you to follow it for any length of time. I would soon re-appear after my death and tell you to take another road. But if I do not return, believe me when I tell you that we never have too much confidence in the good Lord who is so powerful and merciful. We obtain from Him as much as we hope for."[23]

Thérèse did not return to correct her teachings. But she did appear to the Mother Prioress of a Carmel in Gallipoli on the night between the 15th and 16th of January in 1910 during which time she proclaimed, "My Way is sure!"

The suspicion about Thérèse and her teachings continued after her death.

"What authority had this nun who had died after only a few years spent in a monastery? Was her teaching to be accepted in

---

23 Quoted in *The Complete Spiritual Doctrine of St. Thérèse of Lisieux*, pg. 20

preference to that of the masters of the spiritual life and learned theologians? But there were others who, carefully examining Thérèse's words, recognized in them an echo of the Gospel and of the voice of God," writes Fr. Francois Jamart, OCD.[24]

Opposition to her teaching soon died away, especially in the wake of a plethora of miracles ranging from inexplicable healings to the conversion of the hardest of hearts.

So, if you are one of those souls who is tempted to ask, "What can God do with someone as pathetic as me?" you are the perfect candidate for the Little Way whose author had exactly the opposite view.

As you will soon learn, the weaker and more pathetic we are, "the more we attract God"[25] who is only too happy to lend us His strength!

---

24 The *Complete Spiritual Doctrine of St. Thérèse of Lisieux*, pg. 16
25 Quoted in Jamart, Rev. Francois OCD, *Complete Spiritual Doctrine of St. Thérèse of Lisieux* (Staten Island, NY: *Alba House*) 1961, pg. 36

Humility

The Little Way of Spiritual Childhood is not the way of the proud. There is no place in it for the boastful, the grandiose, the powerful. No, the Little Way is the way of *les tout-petits,* the very little ones, that is, those who understand what it means to be truly humble.

With her trademark simplicity, St. Thérèse gives us a very plain and uncomplicated definition of authentic humility:

"It is to recognize our nothingness . . ."[26]

This means that we know who we are – and who we are not.

Does it sound simple? Of course! But just because something is simple, does not make it easy. Recognizing our nothingness is not something we humans like to do. We have a bad habit of trying to be bigger and better than we really are, for a variety of reasons - insecurity, the need to please, to feel good about ourselves, etc.

But this attitude is diametrically opposed to the Little Way. In fact, we should be forever striving to be "littler" rather than "bigger."

So what exactly does it mean to be "little"?

---

26 Clarke, John OCD, *St. Thérèse of Lisieux: Her Last Conversations* (Washington, DC: *ICS Publications*) 1972, pg. 138

"To be little is not attributing to oneself the virtues that one practices, believing oneself capable of anything, but to recognize that God places this treasure in the hands of His little child to be used when necessary; but it remains always God's treasure," Thérèse explains. "Finally, it is not to become discouraged over one's faults, for children fall often . . . "[27]

This littleness, this humility, puts us in our right place, in our true condition, which is why Thérèse makes humility the basis of her Little Way. She believed that humility is truth, and that only the humble can see the truth in all things. But what is this truth that is so elusive that only the truly humble can see it?

Again, the answer is exquisitely simple - God.

As Father P. Marie Eugene, OCD explains, wherever humility is found, there is God.

"And everywhere that God is here below, He clothes Himself, as it were, with a garment that conceals His Presence from the proud and reveals it to the simple and the little ones. When Jesus came to this world, it was as an infant wrapped in swaddling clothes. That was the sign given to the shepherds: 'And this shall be a sign to you,' the angel said, 'you will find an infant wrapped in swaddling clothes and lying in a manger.'[28] The sign of humility always marks the Divine here below."[29]

Which is why, as Thérèse explains, "the lower we are, the more we attract God."[30]

And in her mind, there was absolutely nothing wrong with any condition that might attract God - no matter how embarrassing.

"If I am humble, I am entitled, without offending the good Lord, to do small foolish things until I die. Look at little children. They constantly break things, tear them up, fall, and all the while, in spite of that, they love their parents very much. Well, when I fall

27 Ibid, pg. 139
28 Luke 2:12
29 P. Marie Eugene, OCD, *I Want to See God: A Practical Synthesis of Carmelite Spirituality, Vol. 1* (Allen, TX: *Christian Classics*) 1953, pg. 387
30 Quoted in Jamart, Rev. Francois, OCD, *Complete Spiritual Doctrine of St. Thérèse of Lisieux* (Staten Island, NY: *Alba House*) 1961, pg. 36

in this way, like a child, it makes me realize my nothingness and my weakness all the better, and I say to myself: "What would become of me? What would I be able to accomplish if I were to rely on my own powers alone?"[31]

Just for clarification, Thérèse is not saying that it's okay to sin or to excuse deliberate faults. What she's describing here are moments when we fall even though we are trying our best not to do so.

As Thérèse explains "It is only when His children ignore their constant lapses and make a habit of them and fail to ask His pardon that Christ grieves over them."[32]

Those who follow the Little Way must always be striving to please God but when we do fall, we use those falls to deepen our humility. If we follow this simple rule, we will actually gain more than if we had never fallen. This is because our faults make us realize how weak we are, the extreme need we have of God, and the danger we run in trusting ourselves. In this way our faults keep us humble.

Thérèse uses the example of St. Peter to prove this point.

"I understand very well why St. Peter fell. Poor Peter, he was relying upon himself instead of relying only upon God's strength. . . I'm very sure that if St. Peter had said humbly to Jesus: 'Give me the grace, I beg you, to follow you even to death,' he would have received it immediately."[35]

Not only is this humility - look at the confidence in this statement! This is another hallmark of the Little Way that will be the subject of our next lesson.

But first, we need to practice "acknowledging our nothingness" by accepting the fact that we rarely do so. To one degree or another, we all have a tendency to believe we're trusting in God rather than in our own abilities when, in reality, we're doing the exact opposite.

---

31 *Her Last Conversations*, pg. 140
32 Quoted in *Complete Spiritual Doctrine of St. Thérèse of Lisieux*, pg. 41 [35] Ibid

For instance, how many times have we struggled to overcome a temptation to overeat, to vent on a coworker, to watch prurient shows or movies, only to fall over and over again? We confess these sins every month, determined to do better, but even with our best intentions, we keep falling. Trust in self is most likely the culprit behind these repeated falls. We're just not depending on God the way we ought.

We can spot this self-reliance by examining how we respond to a fall. While it's natural for a first-reaction to be disappointment or shame, if we spend hours tormenting ourselves over it, even out of an intention to "punish ourselves" for the fault, this could be a sign that we're not acknowledging our nothingness. It could very well be that we are so shocked and disturbed by the fall because we secretly have a higher opinion of ourselves and are stunned to learn just how weak we really are.

In the Little Way, there is no such anxiety or despondence.

"I have many weaknesses," Thérèse freely admits, "but I am never astonished because of them."[33]

Instead, she made a prayer out of her falls!

"We would like never to fall. What an illusion! What does it matter, my Jesus, if I fall at every moment? I come to recognize by it how weak I am and that is gain for me. You see by that how little I am able to do and You will be more likely to carry me in your arms. If you do not do so, it is because You like to see me prostrate on the ground. Well, then, I am not going to worry, but I will always stretch out my suppliant arms toward you with great love. I cannot believe that you would abandon me."[34]

Likewise, les tout-petits are not be surprised when they commit a fault because they know how weak they are, and how prone they are to try to "do it" themselves rather than trust in God's help. Rather than succumb to this secret pride, Thérèse would immediately repent of her mistake and run straight into the arms of Jesus who she knew would help her do better next time.

---

33 Quoted in *The Complete Spiritual Doctrine of St. Thérèse of Lisieux*, pg. 39)
34 Ibid

Even as a child she was like this. She once accidentally tore off a piece of wallpaper and couldn't wait until her father came home later in the day to confess her crime. As soon as he walked in the door, she told her sister, "Oh Marie, quickly! Go tell Papa I tore the paper!" As her mother described in a letter, "She awaited her sentence as if she were a criminal. There is an idea in her little head that if she owns up to something, she will be more readily forgiven."[35]

This "idea in her little head" would one day become an integral part of her Little Way and would reflect both the humility and the confidence in God that this spiritual path requires.

"Let us humbly take our place among the imperfect. Let us consider ourselves little and in need of God's support at every instant. As soon as He sees that we are truly convinced of our nothingness, He extends His hand to us. If we are still trying to do something great, even under the pretext of zeal, our good Lord Jesus leaves us alone."[36]

Some might be tempted to be troubled by a fall, thinking it proves that they just don't love God enough, but even this was not an excuse for Thérèse.

As she explains, the humble are "entitled" to do small foolish things because this is due to their weakness, not to any evil intent. Little ones are constantly breaking and tearing things by accident, but this has nothing to do with how much they love their parents. Little children love their parents regardless of their weaknesses. Thérèse suggests that the humble should regard these unwitting falls as reminders of their nothingness, of their weakness, and of how incapable they are of doing anything good without God's help. She asks, "What would I be able to accomplish if I were to rely on my own powers alone?" [37]

---

35 Clarke, John OCD, *Story of a Soul: The Autobiography of St. Thérèse of Lisieux* (Washington DC: ICS Publications) 1972, pg. 19
36 Letter to Sister Genevieve, June 7, 1897
37 Quoted in *The Complete Spiritual Doctrine of St. Thérèse of Lisiuex*, pg. 40

Whenever we fall through weakness and not through a lack of good will, our imperfections do not offend Jesus and do not prevent us from loving Him.

Others might be prone to blame their falls on physical causes such as illness or the weather rather than attribute it to their own imperfection. Although illness and other external forces can indeed influence our minds and moral conduct, Thérèse warns us not to lose sight of the fact that God always grants the graces necessary to overcome all obstacles when we have recourse to Him – even external conditions.

As Father Jamart explains, "Further, she warns us that if we take refuge behind physical infirmities, to excuse ourselves for our imperfections and our falls, we run the risk of overlooking our personal responsibility for them. She wants us rather to recognize that responsibility and to confess that, when we have fallen, it is because we did not have a recourse to prayer as we should have had, or because we have been wanting in generosity. We are then closer to the truth and that is wholly to our advantage."[38]

In other words, no matter why we fall, we must fall "as children," which is through weakness and not a lack of good will.

Accepting our littleness isn't the end of Thérèse's teaching on humility. It's only the beginning!

We are not to be satisfied with just seeing ourselves as we really are. Oh no! That is not nearly far enough for the *les tout-petits*. They must learn how to *love* their nothingness.

"I am not always as prompt as I should like to be in rising above the insignificant things of this world. For example, I might be inclined to worry about some silly thing I have said or done. I then recollect myself for a moment and say: 'Alas, I am still at the point from which I started.' But I say this with great peace and without sadness. It is truly sweet to feel weak and little." [39]

---

38 Ibid, pg 40
39 Clarke, John OCD, *St. Thérèse of Lisieux, Her Last Conversations*, (Washington DC: ICS Publications, 1977) pg. 73-74

Being confronted with our weaknesses is not something most of us feel good about. So how do we accomplish this feat?

Again, it's very simple. Instead of focusing on the weakness, focus on the fact that this is precisely what attracts God to you. And when God is helping you, think of all that you're capable of accomplishing that you could never hope to achieve without Him! It's easy to love our weaknesses once we understand how much more help from God those weaknesses entitle us to.

Over and over again in Scripture God tells us this very same truth.

"'My grace is sufficient for you, for power is [40]made perfect in weakness.' I will rather boast most gladly of my weaknesses, in order that the power of Christ may dwell with me."[43]
We see this truth most dramatically in the story of Gideon, who considered himself to be the least in his family, and yet was called upon by the Lord to defend the Israelites from a powerful army of Midianites. When Gideon protested, the Lord, said, "I will be with you and you will cut down Midian to the last man."[41]

Gideon obeyed and gathered to himself the largest army he could muster and went out to meet the enemy with its much more formidable force.

However, as Gideon was approaching the enemy's camp, the Lord stopped him and said, "You have too many solders with you for me to deliver Midian into their power, lest Israel vaunt itself against me and say, 'My own power saved me."[42]

Gideon was told to ask the soldiers if any were afraid. All those who admitted fear were told to depart. Twenty-two thousand of the soldiers left and only ten thousand remained.

Once again, the Lord told him there were too many soldiers and told Gideon to lead the remaining soldiers to the river and

40 Corinthians 12:9
41 Judges 6:16 (RSV)
42 Judges 7:2

whoever lapped up water with his tongue like a dog could stay. Any soldier who knelt down to drink was banished. This left just three hundred soldiers.

The Lord then said to Gideon: "By means of the three hundred who lapped up the water I will save you and deliver Midian into your power."[43]

It's easy to see what the Lord was doing to Gideon. He was deliberately weakening him by stripping him of his army. And only when he had so few soldiers left that he could not possibly boast over the impending victory did the Lord send him into battle.

Humility does this to us – it weakens us. And this weakening is a kind of death to self that gives the Lord more room in our soul for Him to act. If we're constantly trying to do it ourselves, the Lord has no room to work. Instead, our feeble, fumbling efforts are just getting in the way of the far greater things He has in store for us.

Like St. Paul and Gideon, Thérèse learned how to glory in her weaknesses.

She once wrote to her cousin, "You are mistaken, my dear friend, if you imagine that your little Thérèse walks with ardor in the path of virtue. She is feeble, very feeble. She feels that weakness every day; but Jesus is pleased to teach her the science of glorying in her infirmities. That is a great grace and I pray Jesus to teach it also to you, for there alone are found peace and repose of heart."[44]

Thérèse saw no reason to hide her weaknesses from others, even though most of us are loathe to leave ourselves so exposed to the criticism of others.

Not Thérèse!

---

43 Ibid 7:7
44 Letter addressed to Marie Guerin, July 1890, quoted *in Complete Spiritual Doctrine of St. Thérèse of Lisieux* pg 42.

"That they find you imperfect is precisely what you need," she once instructed her novices. "That is a real blessing, for you can then practice humility which consists not only in thinking and saying that you are full of faults, but in rejoicing because others think and say the same thing about you."[45]

In Thérèse's eyes, this is all necessary if we are to become truly little. She constantly strove to accept all of the humiliations that came her way in life - the snide comments that hurt her feelings, the misunderstandings, the injustice, the betrayals. She used to call these things her "vinegar salads" and was always careful not to let anyone know that her feelings were hurt because she didn't want to draw attention to herself.

She even used unjust criticism to her advantage by saying that she would use them to humble herself with thoughts of how capable she was of doing whatever she had been accused of!

Little ones are also not discouraged when their weaknesses seem to be never-ending.

As Thérèse notes, "In order to belong to Jesus, we must be little, but there are few souls who aspire to remain in that littleness."[46]

After a time, we can become disheartened by constantly relapsing into the same faults and imperfections. Must we be forever small and powerless?

Yes – if God so wills.

"Indeed, it is painful to be constantly confronted with our miseries. But, if God considers it right to leave them with us, is it right for us to complain," Father Jamart asks. "Does He not know better than we do what things are profitable to our soul? These repeated falls, moreover, are often necessary to make us know ourselves better, to convince us of our need of divine help, and teach us humility of heart."[50]

---

45 *The Complete Spiritual Doctrine of St. Thérèse of Lisieux*, pg. 42
46 Letter to Celine, April 25, 1893, quoted in *The Complete Spiritual Doctrine of St. Thérèse of Lisieux*, page 43. 50 Ibid

This doesn't mean that we just throw up our hands and say, "Why bother? I might as well stop trying because God obviously doesn't want to help me correct this fault."

The truly humble soul would never risk consenting to an imperfection in this way. As Father Jamart advises, as long as those falls displease us, they cannot do us harm.

Instead, when we are feeling discouraged by our repeated falls, we must refocus our attention on Jesus rather than dwelling on our imperfections.

"If you are nothing, do not forget that Jesus is
All. Hence, lose your little nothingness in His infinite
All and think only of that *All*, who alone is lovable."[47]

This advice is in keeping with the simplicity that sweetened Thérèse's humility. In contrast with so many who look upon the way of perfection as a complicated and arduous path filled with harsh penances and meticulous exercises, her idea of achieving perfection – or perfect humility – was the exact opposite.

"Perfection seems easy to me. I realize that it is sufficient that we acknowledge our nothingness and abandon ourselves like a child into the arms of our good Lord."[48]

This makes perfect sense to those who want to walk the way of spiritual childhood because children are simple by nature. They're simple in their thoughts, in the way they express themselves, in the way they act. The child says exactly what it thinks because it hasn't yet learned how to be duplicitous.

The childlike soul is also simple. It is not complicated by egoism, self-love, attachments to this and that. Its conduct is simple. It does what it should without pretense. It exists solely for God, leans on Him at every moment. and seeks to please Him in all that it does.

---

47 Letter to Marie Guerin, July 1890
48 Letter addressed to Father Rouland, quoted in *The Complete Spiritual Doctrine of St. Thérèse of Lisieux*, pg. 134.

This seeking to please Him in all that we do - this singular intention of our heart - is what protects us from the sin of presumption.

Thérèse believed this way to sanctity was a perfect fit for *les tout-petits*.

Holiness does not consist of this or that practice, she writes, "but it is a certain disposition of the heart which makes us humble and small as we rest in God's arms, which makes us realize our weakness but, at the same time, gives us confidence to the point of audacity in the goodness of God as our Father."[49]

Everything about the Little Way, even the pursuit of the loftiest virtue of humility, must be simple so as to make it accessible to little souls whose lives consist of the ordinary and the commonplace.

After all, being the Queen of the very little ones, she exemplified what it means to be a very little soul, to be someone who can offer only the smallest and most insignificant things to God.

Which should not embarrass us because "God has no need for brilliant deeds, for beautiful thoughts . . . It is neither intelligence nor talent He is looking for on earth. He loves simplicity. We would indeed deserve pity if we were required to do great things."[50]

As Father Jamart explains, "Nothing is insignificant or negligible in the service of God; for definitely the value of an action does not come from the importance of its object. It comes from the intention with which we perform it and the love with which it is animated."[51]

Instead, "Little things done out of love are those that charm the Heart of Christ . . ."[52]

---

49 *Last Conversations*, pg. 129
50 Quoted in *The Complete Spiritual Doctrine of St. Thérèse of Lisieux*, pg
51 Ibid, pg. 139
52 Letter to Leonie, July 12, 1896

For example, when she first entered the Carmel of Lisieux she tried to mortify herself at meals by mingling bitter herbs with the foods she liked the most, but eventually realized that "it was

more in conformity with the virtue of simplicity to offer them to the good Lord and thank Him for the things which I found to my taste."[53]

There was no better rule than to "follow what love inspires us to do from moment to moment, with the sole desire of pleasing the good Lord in everything He asks of us."[54]

For that matter, in Thérèse's Little Way, even nothingness can be made into an offering.

"If I felt that I had nothing to offer to Jesus, I would offer Him that nothing."[55]

Seeing ourselves, and learning how to love ourselves, as we truly are, teaches us how to live in right relation to God as well as to ourselves and others. And to do this, we need to learn how to be gentle with ourselves.

As Father Jacques Philippe points out, "If we accept ourselves as we are, we also accept God's love for us. But if we reject ourselves, if we despise ourselves, we shut ourselves off from the love God has for us, we deny that love. If we accept ourselves in our weakness, our limitations, it will also be easier for us to accept other people."[56]

This is because those who cannot get along with themselves usually can't get along with others either. People who are unhappy with themselves over their faults or failures tend to get as annoyed with others as they do with themselves.

"Most of our conflicts with others are nothing more than a projection of the conflicts we are having with ourselves."[57]

---

53 Quoted in *The Complete Spiritual Doctrine of St. Thérèse of Lisieux*
54 Ibid
55 Letter to Mother Agnes, January 7-8, 1889
56 Philippe, Father Jacques, The Way of Trust and Love (New York, NY: Scepter Publishers, 2012) pg. 49
57 Ibid

Jesus instructs us to "love your neighbor as yourself"[58] but how can we do that if we don't love ourselves?

In order to fulfill this mandate, we must learn a new and gentler way to look upon our faults and failings.

"The more we accept ourselves as we are and are reconciled to our own weakness, the more we can accept other people and love them as they are."[59]

To be this little and to love this littleness for the sake of loving God requires an enormous amount of trust in Him whom we are striving to please.

"It is confidence and confidence alone that should lead us to love," Thérèse advises.[60]

Thérèse's confidence in God was bold to the point of being audacious. In our next lesson, we will explore this holy boldness that enables the *les tout petits* to become the little giants of sanctity.

---

58 Mark 12:31
59 Ibid
60 Letter addressed to Sister Genevieve, September, 1896

My Little Way Journal

1. Now that you understand the true depth and meaning of the "little" in the Little Way, what emotions does this concept stir in you? Fear? Vulnerability? Incredulity? Amazement? Explain.

   _____
   _____
   _____
   _____
   _____
   _____
   _____

2. In what ways are you living the way of spiritual childhood? In your acceptance of your faults, in your realization of how much you need God? What aspects of spiritual childhood are the most challenging to you at this point in your journey to God? Compose a short and simple prayer asking God to give you the grace to meet these challenges.

   _____
   _____
   _____
   _____
   _____
   _____
   _____

3. Recall the story of how God weakened Gideon by depleting his army. What are your "armies"? What do you need to be stripped of in order for God to work more effectively in you? (For example, your need to feel holy, to look holy, to live up to *your* idea of what a saint should be?)

   _____
   _____
   _____
   _____
   _____
   _____
   _____

4. List a few of the typical excuses you use when confronted with repeated shortcomings. Do you blame others? Do you blame the circumstances of your life for these falls? Ask God to give you the grace to discern what fault may lie within you, and to help you to understand how much you need Him to overcome these imperfections.

_____

_____

_____

_____

_____

_____

5. How might you be over-complicating your spiritual life? Are you making too many demands on yourself with penances, rote prayers, sacrifices? What are the intentions that motivate these demands? Is it love for God or, perhaps, a desire to prove to God and yourself how much you can do for Him? How might the application of Thérèse's teachings on simplicity impact the demands you are currently making on yourself?

_____

_____

_____

_____

_____

_____

6. The Little Way of Spiritual Childhood all comes down to one thing – love. Take some time to examine the intentions behind your actions. How much are you doing for God – and how much for yourself? Ask St. Thérèse to help you to purify your motives so that you might one day live for God alone.

_____

_____

_____

_____

_____

_____

7. How gentle are you with yourself, particularly when you fall? Are you abusive and harsh and unforgiving? Do you say things to yourself that you would never dare to say to another? God treats your faults and failings the way He treated the Prodigal Son – with mercy and compassion. In what ways might you respond to yourself more like this in the future? Compose a short prayer asking God to give you the grace to love yourself as He loves you so that you might, in turn, become a better and more loving neighbor to others.

Confidence

" . . . [T]o look for everything from God as a little child looks for everything from his father."

Could there be a simpler definition of confidence in God?

If humility is the core of St. Thérèse's Little Way, then confidence is its heart. This makes perfect sense because one cannot trust someone – to the point of putting their life in that person's hands - unless they are certain of them with the kind of certainty that can only come from love.

This was definitely the case with Thérèse. She had an unbounding faith in God as her Father and, even in her darkest hours - when she was dying of tuberculosis and suffering through a dreadful dark night of the soul at the same time – she refused to believe that God would ever abandon her.

"Jesus will tire sooner of making me wait than I shall tire of waiting for Him,"[61] she once said, with her characteristic audacity.

Much of her confidence in God was founded in her discovery of Him as a Father rather than as a Judge. This was not an easy feat, especially while living during the reign of the religious movement known as Jansenism that was particularly strong in France at the time. Along with its moral rigor and strict asceticism,

---

61 Letter addressed to Mother Agnes, April or May, 1890)

Jansenism taught that only a certain portion of humanity could be saved, and only perfect contrition was acceptable to God. Thus, Thérèse's belief in God as a merciful Father was a radical departure from the prevailing religious sentiment of the day.

Many believe the reason she was able to develop such a filial love for God as Father was because of the great example of her earthly father, St. Louis Martin with whom she was very close. This gentle and devout man, whom she affectionately referred to as her "dear King"[62] exemplified the characteristics of a good father who was devoted and protective but who also provided everything his children needed to grow physically and spiritually.

Is it any wonder she once told her sister, "It is so sweet to call God our Father!"[63]

This strong belief in a Father God who had all the tender qualities of her earthly father no doubt motivated her tremendous confidence in the mercy of God – even in spite of the times in which she lived. She simply could not fathom God as being anything but what He is – "slow to anger and abounding in mercy."[64]

" . . .[E]ven if I had on my conscience all the sins which can be committed, I would go, my heart broken, to repent and throw myself into the arms of Jesus, for I know how much He cherishes the prodigal child who returns to Him."[65]

Yes, it would be easy to experience this kind of certainty if we were all like St. Thérèse who never committed a mortal sin in her entire life, but what about those of us who have?

Her answer to this question is so characteristic of Thérèse: " . . . I feel that if (though this would be impossible) you were to find a soul more weak and little than mine, you would be pleased to

---

62 St. Thérèse of Lisieux, *Story of a Soul: The Autobiography of St. Thérèse of Lisieux,* translated by John Clarke, OCD (Washington, DC: *ICS Publications,* 1972), pg 37
63 Conversation recorded by her sister Celine, *A Memoir of My Sister St. Thérèse,* p. 109, quoted by Father Jacques Phillippe in *The Way of Trust and Love* (New York, NY: *Scepter Publishers,* 2011), pg. 68
64 Psalm 145:8
65 Quoted in *The Complete Spiritual Doctrine of St. Thérèse of Lisieux,* pg. 64   70 Ibid, pg. 63

shower upon it even greater favors, if it abandoned itself to you with complete confidence in your infinite mercy."[70]

In Thérèse's view, we should have confidence in God's mercy not in spite of what we have done or the many weaknesses and imperfections we struggle with every day, but *because* of them!

We must do this because "misery attracts mercy."[66]

Being aware of this essential quality of God, and acting upon it, is what Thérèse describes as "taking Jesus by the Heart."

"Our Lord has one great weakness. He is blind and He really knows nothing about arithmetic. He does not know how to add, but to blind Him and prevent Him from adding the smallest sum . . . you must take Him by his Heart. This is His weak spot."[67]

What is this blind spot, this weak spot, in the heart of God? Our trust in Him.

"It is this confidence which works all miracles,"[68] writes Father Jean du Coeur de Jesus.

The perfect example of God's response to this kind of humility and confidence can be found in the story of the Good Thief who was crucified alongside Jesus. He knew that he deserved his punishment and told the other criminal who was hanging nearby: "And indeed we have been condemned justly, for the sentence we received corresponds to our crimes, but this man has done nothing criminal." Then he turned to Jesus and said, "Jesus, remember me when you come into your kingdom."[69]

And what does Jesus say in reply? "Amen, I say to you, this day you shall be with me in Paradise."[70]

In that instant, a whole life of sin was forgiven and forgotten – and all because of one humble and confident look of repentance toward the Savior.

---

66 Father Jean du Coeur de Jesus, *I Believe in Love* (Petersham, MA: *St. Bede's Publications*, 1974) pg. 17

67 Quoted in *The Complete Spiritual Doctrine of St. Thérèse of Lisieux*, pg 66

68 *I Believe in Love*, pg. 30

69 Luke 23: 40-41

70 Luke 23: 43

"If you look toward Jesus, with the look of the good thief, do you not believe that you will be purified in a moment, in a second, as he was . . .?" Father Jean writes. "Jesus needs nothing but your humility and your confidence to work marvels of purification and sanctification in you. And your confidence will be in proportion to your humility because it is to the extent that we realize our need of Jesus that we have recourse to him, and we sense this need to the extent that we justly realize our unworthiness."[71]

It's impossible to be truly humble without this kind of confidence. It is the only way that we frail and imperfect humans can bear to see ourselves as the weak and vulnerable and dependent creatures that we truly are. It's simply too terrifying. Confidence in the loving mercy of God is an absolute requirement if we are to ever achieve true humility.

But with this confidence, we hold in our hands the very key to the heart of God.

As Thérèse says, "He measures His gifts according to the amount of confidence He finds in us."[72]

In Thérèse's view, it is utterly impossible to have too much confidence in the good Lord who is so powerful and merciful, which is why she believed that "we obtain from Him as much as we hope to receive from Him."[73]

Does the Lord not teach us this Himself when he tells the blind man, "Let it be done to you according to your faith"?[74]

Did He not teach us that "All things, whatsoever you ask, when you pray, believe that you have already received them, and they shall come unto you?"[75]

See how far He wants us to push our confidence, far enough to believe as if we have already received what we asked for!

But this is not how most of us behave. Instead, we act more like the disciples did when they were crossing the lake of Tiberias in

---

71 *I Believe in Love*, pg. 22
72 Quoted in *The Complete Spiritual Doctrine of St. Thérèse of Lisieux*, pg 64
73 Ibid, pg 61
74 Matthew 9:29
75 Mark 11:24

a boat. When a storm picked up and waves began crashing into the boat, they panicked and cried out to Jesus who was asleep in the stern, "Teacher! Do you not care that we are perishing?"[76] Jesus awoke and rebuked not only the wind but also the disciples for how little confidence they showed in Him. "Why are you terrified? Do you not yet have faith?"[77] He demanded.

As Father Jean writes: "I can hear Jesus scolding them with gentleness, but with pain too. 'Why is this? I was in the boat with you – I slept, but I was there – and you were afraid, you were terrified. You doubted either my omnipotence or my love. Do you not know after all who I am, and do you not know after all with what tenderness my Heart watches over you continually?' It is truly such doubt that pains and offends Him most."[78]

Instead, this is the prayer that should come from the heart of a confident soul at such a time: "With you, Jesus, I cannot perish; you are always in the boat with me; what have I to fear? You may sleep; I shall not awaken you. My poor nature will tremble, oh yes! But with all my will I shall remain in peace in the midst of the storm, confident in you."[79]

For many of us, such a prayer comes hard because in spite of our best intentions, we are lacking in the virtue of hope. Even though most of us believe this virtue is all about hoping all will be well, the supernatural virtue of hope is about trusting that God will deliver on His promises.

As Father Gabriel of St. Mary Magdalen explains, the virtue of faith tells us that God is goodness, beauty, wisdom, providence, charity and infinite mercy, but it's the virtue of hope that reassures us that this great God actually belongs to us.

"We look at the infinite God who is perfect and immensely higher than ourself, a weak, miserable creature, and we wonder: *How can I ever reach Him and be united with Him who is so infinitely beyond my capacity?* And hope replies: *You can, for God Himself wishes it; it was for this reason that He created*

---

76 Mark 4:38
77 Ibid vs. 40
78 *I Believe in Love*, pg. 24
79 *I Believe in Love*, pg. 24

you and raised you to the supernatural state, giving you all the help necessary for such an arduous undertaking."[80]

He reminds us that the Council of Trent affirmed that we should all have "a very firm hope – *firmissimam spem* – in the help of God" because He has promised this help to those who love Him and have recourse to Him with confidence.

Notice the conditions for this hope – to love Him and turn to Him with confidence for the help we need. We do not need to be perfect or sinless or extraordinary in any way. All that is required of us is that we love God and we trust in His promise to help us.

"Hope is the virtue of people who know they are infinitely weak and easily broken, and rely firmly on God with utter trust."[81]

Of course, this kind of hope can only come from a radical experience of our poverty, which is what enables us to place our hope in God alone.

"Although He demands our cooperation and our good works, He does not want us to base our confidence on them," Father Gabriel writes. "In fact, after having urged us to do all that is in our power, Jesus added: 'When you shall have done all these things that are commanded you, say: we are unprofitable servants'."[82]

And just as an act of faith is most meritorious when made during a time of doubt, so is hope when it is clung to in times when we wonder why our good God can allow such evil and death and destruction to plague our lives. In those moments when all hope seems to be gone, when our faith is shaken, and our hearts are breaking, one act of hope in God, albeit made through gritted teeth, is worth more than a thousand such acts made during times of joy and gladness.

This is because the theological virtues of faith, hope and charity, are practiced by the will and are not the result of our feelings.

---

80 Father Gabriel of St. Mary Magdalen, *Divine Intimacy* (Rockford, IL: *TAN Books & Publishers*, 1996) No. 246, pg. 735
81 Phillippe, Father Jacques, *Interior Freedom* (New York, NY: *Scepter Publishers*, 2002) pg. 100.
82 *Divine Intimacy*, No. 247, pg. 738

As Thérèse described near the end of her life as she was enduring tremendous doubts of faith, when she sings of the happiness of heaven and the eternal possession of God, she feels no joy in it but this doesn't stop her. Instead, "I sing simply what I want to believe."[83]

Her hope in God was a matter of sheer will and had nothing at all to do with "feeling" as if everything was going to be all right.

Instead, she responded the way Job did when he said, "Although He should kill me, I will trust in Him."[84]

This is why some of the spiritual masters believe that while charity is the greatest of the three theological virtues, hope is actually the most important.

"As long as hope remains, love develops. If hope is extinguished, love grows cold,"[85] Father Phillippe writes, which is why he sees a world without hope as a world without love.

But hope can't stand alone. It needs faith as well.

"A man of faith is not one who believes that God can do everything, but one who believes he can obtain everything from God."[86]

This is precisely what St. Paul meant when he wrote, "I can do all things in him who strengthens me."[87]

When we understand this principle – that the good-intentioned soul can achieve anything it needs from God – it's easy to see how the lack of hope can lead to discouragement. In fact, Thérèse believed that the sorrow that casts us down after a fall is nothing more than "the hurt to our self-love."[88]

"To brood gloomily over our own imperfection paralyses our soul,"[89] she said.

---

83 *Story of a Soul*, pg. 214
84 Job 13:15
85 *Interior Freedom*, pg. 107
86 *Interior Freedom*, pg. 107
87 Philippians 4:13
88 Quoted in The Complete Spiritual Doctrine of St. Thérèse of Lisieux, pg 64
89 Ibid

Father Jamart adds: "It shows us, too, how defective is our trust in God, for to a great extent God comes to our help in proportion to our consent to remain little and to rely on Him."[90]

This discouragement, this feeling of hopelessness, that can come over us during times of difficulty, could also be the result of a kind of secret despair that belies our need to rediscover the virtue of hope.

Remembering that hope is a virtue practiced primarily by the will, Father Philippe tells us that we need to keep our will strong and enterprising. But in order to do that, the will must be animated by desire.

"Desire can only be strong if what is desired is perceived as accessible, possible. We cannot effectively want something if we have the sense that 'we'll never make it.' When the will is weak, we must represent the object so that it again is seen as accessible. Hope is the virtue that effects."[91]

Only in this way can we learn to "hope against hope"[92] with the unshakeable confidence of St. Thérèse of Lisieux.

In his experience, Father Jean said that he knew of some of the most beautiful and committed souls who refused to believe that confidence held such sway over the Heart of Jesus. Indeed, many people argued with him over the years that it was just too beautiful to be true.

He always answers, "Jesus bought at a dear enough price, at the price of all his blood, the right to bring to earth something 'too beautiful'."[93]

Still, they argue. "So what then? He calls me just as I am? I can go to him with all my miseries, all my weaknesses? He will repair what I have done badly? He will supply for all my indigence?"

Father answers, "Yes, provided that you go to Him, that you count on him, that you expect everything of him, that you say with St. Paul *Omnia possum* (Phil 4:13): I can do all things in Him who is my only strength and my only virtue." [94]

---

90 Ibid
91 *Interior Freedom*, pg. 105-106
92 Romans 4:18
93 *I Believe in Love*, pg 35
94 Ibid

To combat these doubts that have such a ruinous effect on our confidence, he recommends this prayer to be used throughout the day: "Jesus, repair what I have done badly, supply for what I have left undone."

We must also be on guard against another tendency to think that Jesus is dissatisfied when we fall. "Oh, how I would like to help you do away with this atmosphere of distrust, and put you forever into an atmosphere of friendship with your friend Jesus, omnipotent Savior, come for the lost children that we are – lost, but found again like the prodigal son – an atmosphere of hope, a family atmosphere in the mutual confidence of Father and child, which will give you a taste on earth of a happiness which is already heavenly."[95]

If only our first instinct would be to run toward our friend Jesus after a fall rather than to run away from Him in shame! What confidence this would show in the saving power of God!

Thérèse believed that the reason her confidence in Him was so audacious was because he had overwhelmed her with His love – something He wants to do to all of us – if we let Him.

"Oh Jesus, let me tell you, in my boundless gratitude, that Your love becomes truly folly. In the presence of such folly, how could I prevent my heart from trying to fly to You? How could I set limits to my confidence? What a pity that I am not able to reveal Your ineffable condescension to all little souls . . ."[96]

Just as it does in any relationship, trust takes time to build. Two friends must meet regularly and talk to get to know one another. It works the same way in prayer. Regardless of how much time we have or do not have, everyone needs a minimum of faithfulness to prayer. Even if it's only ten minutes before bed, regular contact is a must if we expect to develop a trusting relationship with God.

"Faithfulness to prayer requires a lot of effort, but it is worthwhile," writes Father Philippe. "To be faithful to prayer, you need to establish a rhythm, since our lives are made up of rhythms and we need good habits, including established times when we pray, and that's all there is to it. No questioning it: this

---

95 Ibid, pg. 37
96 Letter addressed to Sr. Genevieve, September 14, 1896

is a firm decision we've made. It requires a struggle at the start, but afterward it brings us great joy."[97]

It is also built by reading and absorbing the Word of God. How many of us have resorted to the Bible during a difficult time only to found a verse – or even a single word – that instantly calmed our troubled heart and restored our peace?

This is because Scripture "possesses a power and authority no human words can have, and it can do much to nurture our trust in God," writes Father Philippe.[98]

Making frequent acts of faith are also ways to increase our trust in God. "Faith grows when it is exercised,"[99] particularly in times of distress when we are so tempted to give in to worry and discouragement. In those times, we say to the Lord, "Jesus, I surrender this to you, take care of it," and then we wait for the Lord to act. Sometimes He does so right away; other times it takes years. But the person of faith knows, and believes, that no prayer goes unanswered.

"All of those acts of faith that may seem sterile, with no immediate results that we can see, are like seeds. Those seeds will unfailingly bear fruit in due course. It doesn't matter whether in five minutes or ten years; let's allow God's wisdom to work."[100]

These acts of trust allow us to exercise our faith and when we do so, our faith and trust grow stronger.

One of the most powerful means to build up our trust in God is in the Sacrament of Reconciliation. When attended with the proper disposition, which is true contrition for our sins, this sacrament provides an invaluable first-hand experience of God's love and mercy. Nothing heals the wounded soul faster than the balm of forgiveness.

In a letter she wrote to Father Belliere, one of her two spiritual brothers, Thérèse tells a story about two naughty sons to explain why she trusts so much in God's mercy. When the father comes to punish his sons, one of them runs away in fear and trembling

---

97 *The Way of Trust and Love*, pg. 82
98 Ibid, pg. 71
99 Ibid
100 Ibid, pg. 72

but the other does the exact opposite. He throws himself into his father's arms, tells him that he loves him, and begs for forgiveness. This son goes even further and asks the father not only to punish him for his offenses, but to do so with a kiss.

"I don't think the happy father could harden his heart against his child's filial trust, knowing his sincerity and love," Thérèse writes.[101]

It takes great trust to come before God in this sacrament and ask for forgiveness! And every time we do so, we strengthen our confidence in God even more.

While all of these ways are recommended for building trust, we must be careful to be sure that we are truly trusting in God and not in ourselves.

"Sometimes we are more or less under an illusion about this," Father Philippe warns. "Sometimes we manage to do what is right, lead a good and virtuous life, have great trust in God, without the slightest problem; and then a difficult time comes. ...We are brought face-to-face with our defects, and we become sad and discouraged. All our great trust in God melts away like snow in the sun.

"This simply means that what we called trust in God was in fact trust in ourselves. If trust disappears when we do wrong, it shows that our trust was based on ourselves and our deeds. Discouragement is a clear sign that we've put our trust in ourselves and not at all in God."[102]

This unhappy circumstance can come about if we spend too much time focused on our progress in the spiritual life. We examine every tiny nuance about our behavior, evaluating ourselves and measuring how close we are to achieving perfection.

The usual result of this kind of behavior is to create "a sort of discontent and permanent sadness" to slip into our lives, Father warns, because we are never fully satisfied with ourselves.

The duty of examining our conscience should not be avoided because we need to do this, but we should be careful to avoid

---

101 Quoted in *The Way of Trust and Love*, pg. 96
102 Ibid, pg. 94

allowing this examination to degenerate into "gazing gloomily" at ourselves.

"Such an attitude causes us to center on ourselves when what we need to do is throw ourselves on God with unlimited trust."[103]

For those who want to walk the way of spiritual childhood, we must believe with all of our strength in these words of Jesus: "With God, all things are possible."[104]

103 The Way of Trust and Love, pg. 94
104 Matthew 19:26

My Little Way Journal

1. How have your experienced the mercy of God in your life? How has this impacted your level of trust in God?

_____
_____
_____
_____
_____
_____
_____

2. Do you sometimes feel as if God has done so much for you, and shown so many proofs of His love and mercy, and yet you still do not trust Him as much as you ought? What might be causing you to doubt Him? Make a list and bring it to Him in prayer, asking Him to give you the grace to overcome these impediments.

_____
_____
_____
_____
_____
_____
_____

3. Imagine yourself in the boat with the disciples when the violent winds begin to blow and yet Jesus remains asleep in the stern. How would you act? What does this reveal about your confidence in God?

_____
_____
_____
_____
_____
_____
_____

4. Developing the virtue of hope is a requirement for all those who wish to become more confident in God, but hope isn't about wishing everything will turn out all right. It's about knowing that God is in control and that His will is best. Write down the most difficult circumstance in your life right now – the one thing you would most like to change - and, even if you can barely get the words out, make an act of hope.

_____

_____

_____

_____

_____

_____

_____

5. How do you deal with your imperfections? Do you agonize over them? Do you believe they're just too great to be overcome? Are you tired of trying – and failing – to correct these faults? Could this be causing you to suffer from a kind of "secret despair" about ever achieving Christian perfection, so why try? Regardless of how you regard your imperfections, take a moment to prayerfully renew your faith and trust in God's word when He says that "With God, all things are possible" (Matt 19:26).

_____

_____

_____

_____

_____

_____

_____

6. Which of the suggestions offered for developing more confidence and trust in God most appeals to you? Why? How might you incorporate this practice into your daily life?

_____

_____

_____

_____

_____

_____

_____

Lesson Four

Abandonment

Once again, Thérèse describes the third basic quality of the Little Way with her characteristic simplicity.

> *"It is to be disquieted by nothing."*[105]

But how is this possible for weak human beings such as ourselves, who are beset with a thousand worries a day in our frantic lifestyles, to not be disturbed by anything? We have bills to pay, children to raise, jobs to perform, homes to upkeep. Can anyone really do this?

Yes and no. To be "disquieted by nothing" doesn't mean we will escape all worry or anxiety which would be impossible because these emotions are part of our human condition. What it does mean is that we will not allow ourselves to be *voluntarily* or *deliberately* disturbed.

We must never consciously consent to anxiety or a troubled mind because this means we are worrying with the full consent of the will. Even though our human nature might feel worry and anxiety, our human will is what enables us to consent to it.

This is what Thérèse means when she teaches that we must not allow ourselves to be disquieted by anything. When we feel

---

105 *St. Thérèse of Lisieux: Her Last Conversations*, translated by John Clarke, OCD (Washington, DC: *ICS Publications*, 1977) pg. 138

anxiety and worry pressing in upon us, we make an act of faith and trust in God and surrender to His will for us in whatever circumstance might be assailing us. This behavior can do much to restore our peace of soul and also trains our will to respond correctly in situations of anxiety.

For example, Father Jean du Coeur de Jesus suggests this payer: "Jesus, you are here: nothing happens, not a hair falls from my head, without your permission. I have no right to worry."[106]

When we turn to God in moments like this, it teaches us to rely upon God rather than ourselves and slowly begins to form within us a new attitude of surrender to God.

"Abandonment is confidence which no longer expresses itself solely through distinct acts but has created an attitude of soul . . ."[107]

This attitude was so well-formed in Thérèse that she once declared abandonment to be "my only guide."[108]

"I follow the way traced for me by Jesus . . . He wants me to practice abandonment, like a little child which does not worry about what others might do with Him . . . I try to be no longer occupied with myself in anything and I abandon to Him whatever He wants to accomplish in my soul."[109]

Remember, Thérèse could do this not because she was a giant of a saint but because was the littlest of saints, one who not only acknowledged her nothingness, but embraced it. And because she knew that God was all-merciful, she had perfect confidence that He would supply whatever grace she needed in order to fulfill His will for her. If He wanted her to be holy, and inspired that desire within her own heart, she was confident that He would give her whatever she needed to achieve this goal.

"The good God would not inspire unattainable desires,"[110] she believed.

---

106 *I Believe in Love*, pg. 55
107 *I Am a Daughter of God*, pg 395
108 Quoted in *The Complete Spiritual Doctrine of St. Thérèse of Lisieux*, pg. 126
109 Letter to Abbe Belliere, June 21, 1897
110 Quoted in *I Believe in Love*, pg.16

Even if that meant He had to become what she so famously referred to as her "elevator" who carried her up the steep staircase of perfection. In other words, Thérèse was humble enough to realize she could never achieve holiness without the help of God's grace – the same grace that is available to all of us – and was confident enough to both ask for it and accept His help in whatever form He chose to give it.

This is true abandonment. Not only did she abandon her earthly life to Him, but her eternal life as well.

As Father Jean correctly asserts: " . . . [A]bandonment, rightly understood is the greatest of all renunciations."[111]

This is where most of us differ from Thérèse. We fail to exercise the virtue of hope which enables us to "tear away the veil" and see Jesus behind all the ups and downs of life. We don't see Him and therefore we don't turn to Him and the grace He has ready for us. Instead of being open to His will, "We thwart His plans by imposing our own views, our little plans to which we hold so tightly," writes Father Jean.

Why do we do this? Perhaps because we fear a cross, a suffering, a humiliation, or because we're thirsting for some pleasure or ambition.

God teaches us to " . . . [S]eek first the Kingdom of God and his righteousness"[112] and all these other things will be added unto us; but we don't do this. We seek our own advantage first, our interest, money, etc.

And so, as Father Jean teaches, "Jesus turns away."

He can't help us because we're too busy helping ourselves. We've shut Him out.

This is not the way of *les tout-petits*. Little ones are not afraid to ask their parents for help; neither do they doubt for a minute that their parents will give them the help they need because they are confident in their parents' love for them. As a result, trusting in this love and ready help, they worry about nothing.

---

111 *I Believe in Love*, pg. 19
112 Matthew 6:33

"Such is the child: a being essentially poor and trustful, convinced that its poverty is its most precious treasure."[113]

There is no greater proof of love of God, and confidence in Him, than to abandon ourselves to Him. The good news is that this proof redounds to our benefit.

"Abandonment . . . gives us a better means of realizing our destiny and of attaining the holiness to which we are called. God has special designs regarding each and every soul and He alone knows what they are," writes Father Francois Jamart, OCD.

"When we try to guide ourselves, we risk putting obstacles in the way of divine action as a consequence of our meddling and deviating from the path marked out for us by God; whereas when we abandon ourselves to God, we walk on the safe road. We enter the way that leads most quickly to the goal that He has set for us."[119]

One of the most supreme benefits to abandonment to God is the great peace that it brings in its wake. This is because trusting in the will of God enables a person to be free from the relentless demands of the passions and preferences that bully us throughout our lives. These are our desires for worldly gain and honors, for preferring certain persons to others, for wanting everything to be to our liking so that we don't have to suffer any kind of hardship or discomfort. How earnestly we struggle to make everything turn out the way we want it!

But an attitude of abandonment doesn't think that way. Rather than allowing oneself to be chased to and fro by these desires, true abandonment to God's will allows us to let Him decide the outcome, confident that it is the best one for us. By doing so, we allow God, rather than our passions, to control us.

And, therefore, we have peace.

"I love all that the good Lord gives me," Thérèse loved to say.

---

113 P. Marie Eugene, *I am A Daughter of the Church: A Practical Synthesis of Carmelite Spirituality* (Christian Classics: Allen, TX, 1955) pg. 398 [119] Jamart, Fr. Francois OCD, *The Complete Spiritual Doctrine of St. Thérèse of Lisieux*, (Staten Island, NY: *Alba House*, 1961) pg. 127

However, this doesn't mean that we refrain from using our reason and responding appropriately to the circumstances of our lives. We absolutely must foresee and make plans and act as if it all depended on ourselves.

This is because true abandonment is neither quietism nor fatalism.

"We must devote ourselves to doing all we have to do, with the greatest fidelity, the greatest generosity, notwithstanding, of course, all our weakness . . . Our task is to have worked with all of our good will, in spite of our state of misery, without ever forgetting that Jesus . . . is there to carry us. Then, having acted this way with him, we must never worry over the results. If he wills an apparent failure – I say apparent failure, for a failure willed by God is not a real failure – all is well. 'Thank you, Jesus'," Father Jean advises.

"If He destroys my little plans, I kiss His adorable hand. It is because He wants to realize His own, which are more beautiful anyway than those which I could have made myself. If He permits a very beautiful success – from my viewpoint – 'Thank you again.' (That thank you is much easier to say!)"[114]

Even if we have to consent to God's will in a particular circumstance amidst great resistance, what does it matter? The mere struggle to do so only confirms that we are not consenting to worry or anxiety or discouragement and are doing all within our feeble power to accept God's will.

"All of those movements of our nature, if we do not consent to them, do not exist for Him," Father Jean reassures.[115]

For example, we may entertain proud thoughts from time to time, or strong feelings about how much we want our own will in a particular situation. When we do, we must ask ourselves if we are happy with those thoughts. Do we give them our full consent? Most times we can probably answer, "No, I am not happy with them and feel ashamed of them and try to reject them."

---

114 *I Believe in Love,* pg. 53
115 *I Believe in Love,* pg. 56

In this case, we are not proud because the truly proud person chooses to be proud. This person has no intention of submitting to God's will.

On the other hand, the one who feels badly about such thoughts is merely experiencing the prideful nature that plagues us all. By making acts of humility at such a time, by saying, "God I want so badly to have things turn out my way – but not my will let yours be done" – even if the latter part of the prayer is said without any feelings of submission - we have done all that we can. Jesus will see only our good will, our feeble efforts to please Him, and He will provide the rest.

"We are all sinners, and it is necessary for us to recognize it, beating our breast; but the impenitent sinner is the one who has chosen sin," Father Jean writes.

"We must not think that sanctity is soaring above temptations, difficulties and obstacles. . . We live under a Master who died only to rise again, and we possess the

hope which is the certainty of his victory, a victory which is ours to the extent that we do not separate ourselves from him. We can even rejoice, in a sense, in having an evil nature which justly gives us the occasion
to deny it our consent and to repeat, 'No Jesus, it is your will that I love; it is that which I want and nothing else. It is you whom I choose'."[116]

As he so succinctly puts it: "Abandonment is nothing but obedience pushed to its extreme, since it consists of submission to everything within the limits of the possible and the reasonable, in order to obey God who has foreseen and willed it."[117]

To live this way is to live the Truth because, "all the lines, all the words, and all the letters of our lives"[118] were written by God.

Father Jean tells an interesting story about abandonment to God that involved St. Margaret Mary who brought us the devotion to

116 *I Believe I Love*, pg 57
117 Ibid, pg 50-51
118 Ibid

the Sacred Heart of Jesus. Throughout her lifetime, she would often hear Jesus say to her, "Let me do it."

However, it wasn't until the very end of her life that she realized exactly what He meant by it.

"His Sacred Heart will do everything for me if I let Him. He shall will, He shall love, He shall desire for me and make up for all my faults."[119]

When we are faced with a myriad of problems in our lives, from trying to reason with rebellious children, to dealing with discord in the workplace or parish, and experiencing troubles in our relationships, how many times does Jesus whisper in our ears during the day, "Let me do it?" Instead of turning to Him with confidence and inviting Him into our troubles by saying, "Jesus, I surrender this to you" or some other quick prayer, we stand there wringing our hands and feeling overwhelmed and hopeless.

Thérèse no doubt felt the same kind of raw emotions during her short life, such as when her beloved father was committed to an asylum, but she refused to let go of the belief that her loving Father in heaven knew best.

As dreadful as this circumstance was, on the day of her profession, when she wanted so badly to pray for her father's cure, she could only do so with words couched in her belief in God's loving mercy.

"My God, I beg you, let it be your Will that Papa be cured!"[120]

History relays the choice God made and her father remained in the asylum until his death. As painful as this was Thérèse, if such a loving Father in heaven chose this fate for her earthly father, how could she not accept it?

"I follow the way traced for me by Jesus," she once wrote. "He wants me to practice abandonment, like a little child which does not worry about what others might do with him . . . I try to be no longer occupied

---

119 Ibid
120 Clarke, John OCD, *St. Thérèse of Lisieux: Her Last Conversations* (Washington DC: *ICS Publications*, 1977) pg. 107

with myself in anything and I abandon to Him whatever He wants to accomplish in my soul."[121]

Because God enabled her to do this, she remained in a state of peace. "My heart is full of the will of God," she once described. "So if anything else were poured over it, it could not even get in. I will remain in a state of peace that nothing can disturb."[122]

Father Jean called abandonment the practical and actual application of an obsession: the will of God.

"That is why certain persons in the world, men of the people, this peasant on his farm, that worker in the factory, are true saints – because they have understood that the will of God is everything and they are disposed to prefer it to everything else. . . This is where the supernatural indifference of the saints comes from: joy or pain, consolation or dryness, light or darkness, adulation or criticism, honey or gall, health or sickness, life or death . . . *Fiat voluntas tua*, Thy will be done."[123]

One of her secrets for accomplishing this great peace was one that all of us are wise to copy – she insisted upon living in the present moment. Why should this matter so much?

Because the present moment is where God is. He is not in the future, or in the past, but is perpetually present.

And wherever God is, there is His grace.

In other words, if we want to live the way of the *les touts-petit*, which is a way only possible with the assistance of God's grace, we must remain in the present where our Help resides.

Thérèse once taught this vital lesson to her novices who came to her one day to voice their concern about how much she was suffering from the tuberculosis that would eventually claim her life. Not only were they upset by what she was suffering on that particular day, they were also disturbed by what suffering may still lay in store for her.

---

121 Quoted in *The Complete Spiritual Doctrine of St. Thérèse of Lisieux*, pg. 126
122 Ibid, pg. 127
123 *I Believe in Love*, pg. 59

" . . . [Y]ou are quite wrong in imagining what painful things might happen to me in the future, for that is like interfering with God's work of creation," she told them. "We must run in the way of love, must never worry about anything. If I did not accept my suffering from one minute to another, it would be impossible for me to remain patient. But I see only the present moment, forget the past and take good care not to visualize the future... To think of the painful things that might happen in the future means that we are lacking in confidence."[124]

How true this is! So many of the great spiritual masters have issued the same warning as Thérèse.

Father Jacques P. de Caussade called these anxious thoughts a temptation from the devil.

"Why are we so skillful in tormenting ourselves beforehand with what will possibly never happen? Sufficient for the day be the evil thereof! Anxious forethought does us much harm; why then do we indulge in it so readily? We are the enemies of our own peace of soul."[125]

Again, this doesn't mean that we refrain from making appropriate plans for our future. We must do whatever is prudent for ourselves and our families. However, we must never allow ourselves to become anxious and worried about the future because, as Thérèse explains, this reveals a lack of confidence in God.

And so, as we come to the end of our study on the Little Way of Spiritual Childhood, it's safe to say that abandonment, rightly understood, embodies the whole of our saint's teaching.

"[Abandonment] requires a great humility, since it is submission of oneself to creatures and events, seeing Jesus himself in them. It requires an immense faith, confidence every moment, to tear open the veil of secondary causes, to break through the screen of creatures which too often prevents us from seeing Jesus behind them, who governs everything, since nothing, nothing happens without his having willed or permitted it."[126]

---

124 Quoted in *The Complete Spiritual Doctrine of St. Thérèse of Lisieux*, pg. 134
125 De Caussade, Jacques P. SJ, *Self-Abandonment to Divine Providence* (Rockford, IL: *Tan Books and Publishers*, 1959), pg. 324
126 *I Believe in Love*, pg. 50

My Little Way Journal

1. Think back to the last time something went seriously wrong in your life. What was your first response? When you prayed to God, did you tell Him how you wanted Him to handle it, or were you able to say "not my will but yours be done"? If you were truly living the Little Way, how might you have handled this situation instead?

_____

_____

_____

_____

_____

_____

_____

2. Surrender to God doesn't mean that we don't plan for our future or take the necessary steps to ensure that our lives are lived out in an orderly fashion. Our problem is that we tend to go too far and spend far too much time worrying about this or that. Jot down a few worries that you would like to turn over to God today, then pray for the grace to do so.

_____

_____

_____

_____

_____

_____

_____

3. Now that you've completed this course on the Little Way, rank yourself with a grade of A-F on how well you live each of the three core elements of the Little Way of Spiritual Childhood - humility, confidence, and abandonment. Take this ranking to prayer and ask God to help you to discern what practical steps you can take today to improve in each of these areas.

_____

_____

_____

_____

_____

_____

_____

4. Compose a personal prayer to St. Thérèse, asking for her help in living the Little Way. Let the prayer come from your heart and be in your own words, then pray it every day as you begin to Live the Little Way in earnest!

_____

_____

_____

_____

_____

_____

_____

About Live Catholic

Live Catholic is a lay-run apostolate founded by Secular Discalced Carmelites from various communities throughout the United States who are devoted to infusing the world with the truth of the Catholic mystical tradition as revealed by the Carmelite saints and Doctors of the Church.

Our aim is to make the teachings of St. Teresa of Avila, St. John of the Cross, St. Thérèse of Lisieux, and other Carmelite saints more accessible and understandable to the faithful. We offer courses explaining St. Teresa's four stages of prayer and the seven mansions of the soul, as well as St. Thérèse's Little Way of Spiritual Childhood. Our courses, workshops and conferences also include instruction on spiritual warfare, discernment, how to acquire Peace of Soul, and a variety of other topics. Courses and workshops are taught in both cohort-based (live instruction) and self-paced learning (provided via Teachables). In addition, these learning materials are offered on-demand, meaning parishes and other small groups can request a course/workshop to be taught on the day/time of their choosing.

All of our courses have an imprimatur from the Archdiocese of Philadelphia and are faithful to the Magisterium and free of any New Age components.

For more information visit www.livecatholic.org or contact us at info@livecatholic.org.

Made in the USA
Middletown, DE
04 July 2023

34331284R00040